John
Beloved Apostle

DOROTHY LAUX • ILLUSTRATED BY WILLIAM N. McPHEETERS

BROADMAN PRESS
Nashville, Tennessee

4242-34
ISBN: 0-8054-4234-0

Dewey Decimal Classification: J225.92
Subject heading: JOHN, APOSTLE
Printed in the United States of America

Contents

A Busy Day

"Wake up sleepyhead," James called as he pulled on his brother's sleeping mat.

John turned over on his mat, opened his eyes, and stretched his arms. Finally, he got up, rolled up his sleeping mat, and put it in the chest.

The boys found their mother taking round loaves of hot bread out of the oven in the courtyard.

"Um-m-m, that smells good," John said as he gave his mother a good-morning hug.

Mother poured the boys a cup of goat's milk and gave them some hot bread and fresh figs to eat.

"Please Mother, may we go to the well with you before time for school?" John pleaded. The boys liked to go to the well because it gave them a chance to see some of their friends.

"I'll race you to the well," John called.

"Okay," James answered.

The children ran races and played games. Their mothers lowered the clay jars into the deep well and filled them with cool, clear water.

"Time to go," mother called to James and John. She balanced the large water jar on her head, and they walked home through the market area.

The brothers looked into each palm-covered booth. They saw farmers measuring and selling grain. One merchant sold clay bowls and water jars. Another merchant sold sleeping mats and material for making tents. Shepherds sold sacks of wool gathered from shearing their

sheep. James and John watched as the fisherman weighed his fish.

"Someday I'll be selling fish in this market," John thought to himself. His father, Zebedee, was already teaching James and John the fishing business.

"Look!" James called as he pointed toward a camel caravan.

"They are probably bringing spices and fine jewels from the East," John said.

"Hurry along, boys," Mother urged. "You must not be late for school."

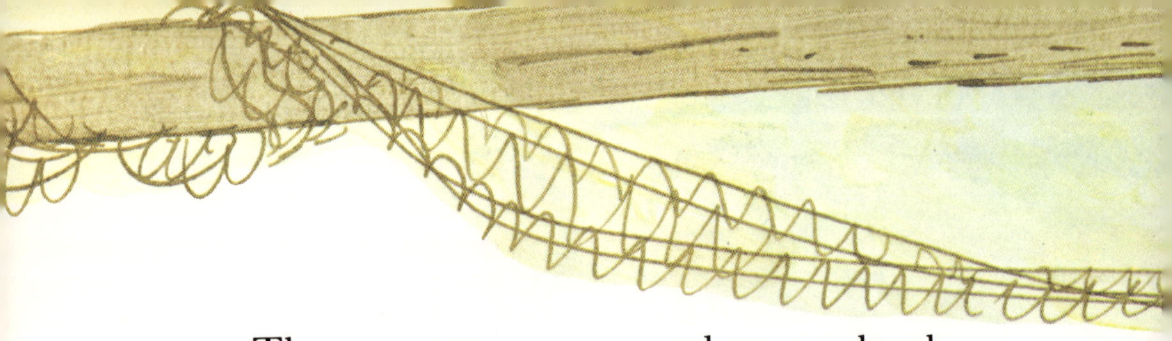

The synagogue was used as a school during the week and as a place of worship on the sabbath.

The class gathered at the feet of the rabbi who sat on a low stool. James and John took their places on the floor with the others. The boys read aloud from the Hebrew scrolls. John's favorite Scripture reading was: "Hear, O Israel: The Lord our God is one Lord: And thou shalt love the Lord thy God with all thine heart, and with all thy soul, and with all thy might." He repeated this Scripture over and over.

After school James and John ran to the seashore to play and to help Zebedee, their father.

Zebedee showed his sons the correct way to cast the net and lower it into the water. As the sun was about to set, Zebedee guided the boat to shore.

"I need your help, boys," he said. "We must hang the nets to dry." The boys pulled and tugged the heavy nets. Finally, the job was finished, and the three headed for home. They carried with them some of the fish they had caught.

The family gathered around the large straw mat on the floor. Mother placed the food on the mat. As they sat cross-legged on the floor, Zebedee thanked God for the food.

After supper Zebedee lit the clay lamp and placed it on a shelf. He took the scroll from the chest and read aloud to his family. Soon it was time for James and John to unroll their sleeping mats and go to bed. It had been a long, busy day for the brothers.

Thinkback: Part of this story is a pretend story. The Bible does not tell us about John's childhood, but we know he grew up in a typical Jewish home. He did the same things other Jewish boys did.

How is your day different from the day in this story? How is it like the one in this story?

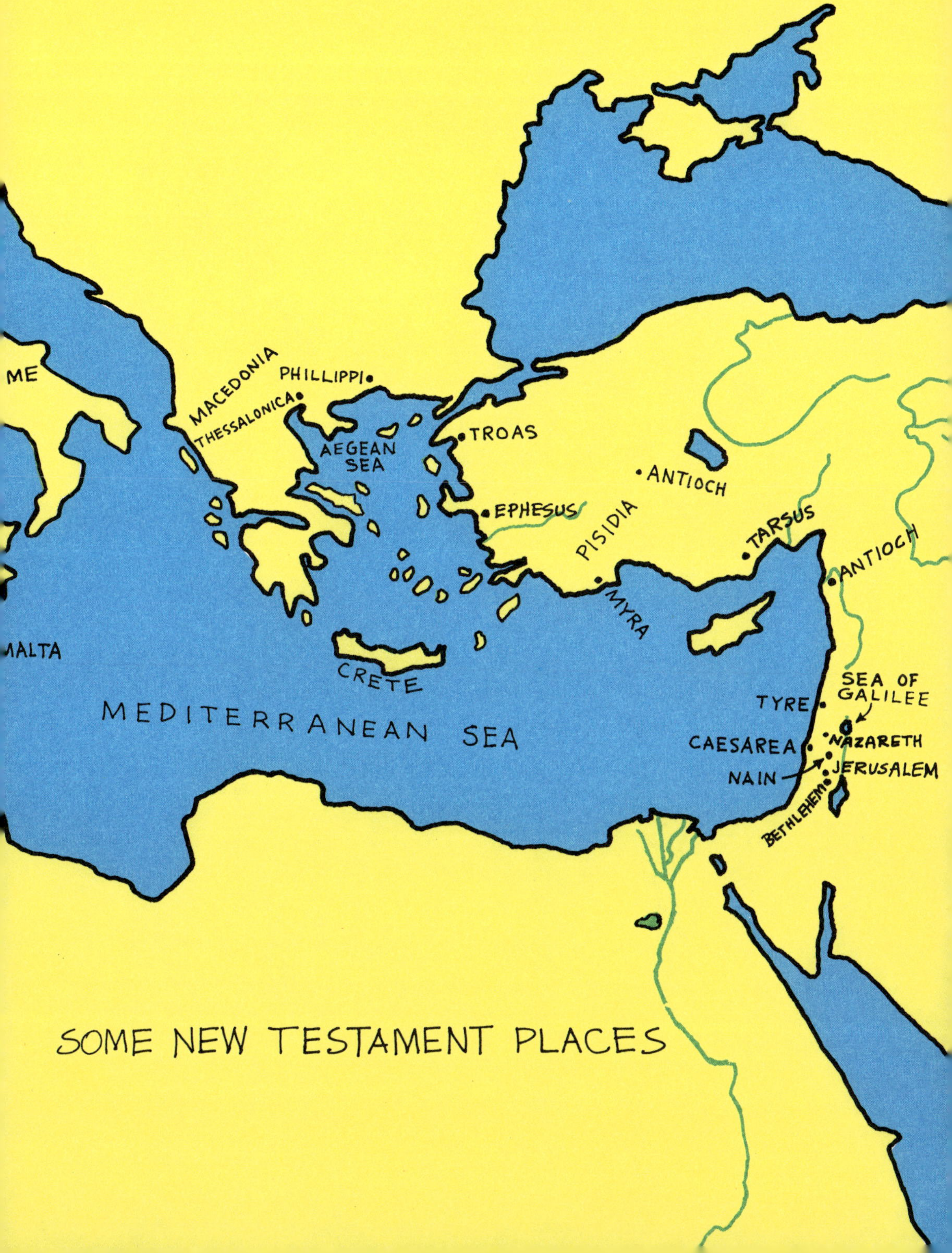

SOME NEW TESTAMENT PLACES

Come, Follow Me

Zebedee was glad when his sons, James and John, were old enough to join him in his successful fishing business. The three men made a good living catching and selling fish.

"Look at all the fishing boats on the lake tonight," John said to Zebedee as they pushed their boat away from the shore.

"I see our friends Peter and Andrew are already on the lake," James added.

Zebedee knew all the good places to cast fishing nets. He knew that night was the best time to set sail for fishing. The fishermen went back and forth over the dark blue waters casting their heavy nets.

The nets settled on the water and the lead weights pulled the nets under the water. When the net was full of fish, one quick pull by the fishermen closed the net like a sack, trapping the fish.

John waved across the water to his friends Peter and Andrew. "Have you caught anything?" John called.

"Not a thing," came the reply.

"It's been a long, hard night," Zebedee said to his sons as they sat in the boat mending their nets. "Let's quit and go home."

Before they could reply the men heard someone calling, "John, James." They turned and saw Jesus standing on the shore.

"Come, follow me," Jesus called, "and I will make you fishers of men. I want you to be my helpers. Everyday you will be with me as I teach and preach."

Immediately John and James left their nets and followed Jesus.

Thinkback: Do you think John was a good fisherman? Why?

How do you think Zebedee felt when his sons left their nets to follow Jesus?

Jesus Trains John

John and James were ambitious, eager, and fiery young men. Knowing this, Jesus gave John and James the nickname *Boanerges,* which means "sons of thunder." Jesus liked John's youthful enthusiasm. Often Jesus had to control John's actions. Jesus wanted to teach the young men how to be good disciples.

One day John suggested harsh punishment for a village that had refused hospitality to Jesus. "Lord, command fire to come down and burn their city," John demanded.

Jesus promptly replied, "No, John, I have come not to destroy people but to save them."

Many times John was impatient. He always wanted to be first in everything.

He and James were even selfish in requests they made of Jesus.

One day they had their mother speak to Jesus for them. "Please, Lord, give my sons the places of honor and power in your kingdom. Let one sit on your right and one on your left."

Jesus replied, "You don't even know what you are asking."

When the other disciples found out

about this request, they were filled with anger. "Who do they think they are?" they asked one another.

Jesus patiently gathered his disciples around him. He made a simple but important statement to them. "In my kingdom a man becomes great by being the servant of others."

Jesus continued to teach and train John and the other disciples.

He taught them lessons in:

humility, when he washed the disciples' feet.

forgiveness, when he said, "Forgive seventy times seven times."

giving, when he saw the woman give two small coins and he said, "This woman has given more than all the others because she has given all she has."

prayer, when the disciples came and asked, "Lord, teach us to pray."

love, when he said, "Do not send the children away, bring them to me."

sharing, when he met the Samaritan woman at the well and told her the good news of eternal life.

Thinkback: Jesus wanted John to learn many lessons. What were four of these?

Jesus wants you to learn these same lessons. How many have you already learned?

It's a Miracle

"Come with me," Jesus said to James and John. Jesus was on his way to Peter's home.

"My mother is very sick," Peter's wife told Jesus as he entered the house. "Can you help?" she asked.

Jesus entered the room, took the sick woman by the hand and raised her up. Immediately the fever left her. John saw Jesus use his power to heal Peter's mother-in-law.

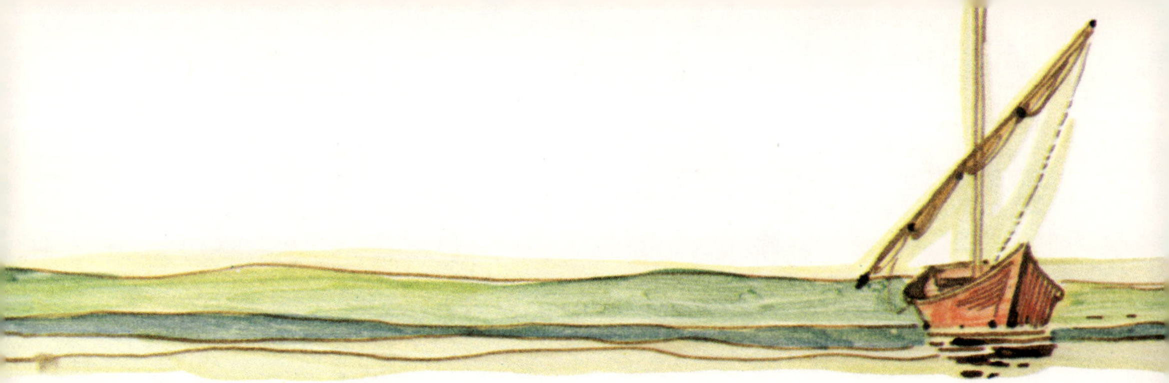

Later John and the other disciples saw a leper run toward Jesus. The leper fell on his face at Jesus' feet and said, "Lord, I know you can heal me if you will."

Jesus reached out and touched the leper. Jesus said, "I will help you. You are well. Go be with your friends." John and the other disciples stood amazed as Jesus quietly healed the leper.

Jesus and his disciples entered many towns and villages. One day as they came to the city of Nain they met a funeral procession. A large crowd was in the procession. Jesus felt sorry for the widow whose son had died. Jesus spoke softly, "Woman, do not cry." He stopped the procession and said, "Young man, get up."

All of those present watched with wonder as the young man sat up and began to speak.

"It's a miracle," John whispered quietly to his brother James.

Sometimes Jesus and the disciples walked when they traveled. Other times they crossed to another place by boat. The disciples liked to be alone in the boat with Jesus.

One day Jairus, a ruler in the synagogue, met Jesus by the sea. "My little girl is dying. Please come and lay your hands on her. I know you can make her live."

While Jairus spoke, a servant came and said: "Your child is dead. Don't trouble the master."

Jesus said to Jairus, "Don't worry. If you will only believe, she will live."

Jesus took John, James, and Peter with him to the home of Jairus. Jesus took the girl by the hand and said, "Little girl, get up." Immediately the girl got up and walked.

Peter, James, and John were astonished. They could hardly believe what they had seen with their own eyes.

Walking along the roadway with his disciples Jesus came upon a blind beggar named Bartimaeus. The beggar called out, "Jesus, help me."

Someone in the crowd said to Bartimaeus, "Be quiet. Don't bother Jesus."

"Bring him to me," Jesus commanded. "Bartimaeus, your faith has made you whole," Jesus said. Immediately the blind man could see. When John and the others saw what had happened they praised God.

Thinkback: Name at least three of the miracles you read about. How do you think you would have felt if you had seen Jesus perform a miracle?

How many other miracles of Jesus can you remember? Tell a friend about one of Jesus' miracles.

Great Moments with Jesus

Large crowds followed Jesus wherever he went. Many pushed close to listen as he spoke. Others brought the sick, lame, and blind to be healed. Jesus sometimes became tired and weary. Once he got into a boat with his disciples to cross the Sea of Galilee. Immediately Jesus went to sleep.

A storm came up on the lake. "It looks like the boat will be torn apart," John said to Peter as he gripped the side of the boat.

"Maybe we can keep it under control," Peter called as he worked with the oars.

"Where is Jesus?" someone asked.

"He's asleep," came the reply.

"Wake him up before the boat sinks."

"Master, don't you care that we are all

about to drown?" they asked.

Jesus woke up and saw what the disturbance was all about. He said to the wind and waters, "Peace, be still." The wind stopped blowing. The lake became calm.

Jesus looked at his disciples and said, "Why were you so afraid? Don't you have any faith?"

John thought Jesus looked straight at him as he spoke. The disciples said to one another, "What kind of man is Jesus? Even the winds and the waves obey him."

John liked to be near Jesus. Wherever Jesus went and whatever he was doing, John wanted to be with him.

Jesus took John and Peter and James up to a high mountain. While they were on the mountain a strange thing happened. They did not understand it. A great change came over Jesus. His clothes became white and his face glowed like the sun. The three disciples watched in wonder and astonishment. Moses and Elijah appeared and talked with Jesus.

Suddenly a cloud came over all of them. They heard a voice out of the cloud say, "This is my own Son—listen to him."

Peter, James, and John fell on their faces. They were afraid. Jesus touched them and said, "Don't be afraid." When they got up they were alone with Jesus. John knew this was an important time in the life of Jesus.

Excitement filled the city of Jerusalem. The Passover feast was near. People crowded into the city. Everyone talked about Jesus. Some asked, "What do you think of him? Where is he?"

At that very moment Jesus was getting ready to enter the city. John helped Jesus get on the back of the borrowed donkey. Jesus smiled at John. Somehow they always seemed to understand each other. John walked beside Jesus. Occasionally John glanced lovingly into the Master's face.

As they entered Jerusalem the streets were filled with people. There was a feeling of excitement in the air. People waved palm branches and spread their coats on the ground where Jesus passed. They cried out, "Blessed is he that comes in the name of the Lord. Hosanna in the highest."

John looked at Jesus again. "Truly this is a great hour," John thought to himself. He did not know the troubled times that were ahead.

Thinkback: Recall three great moments John shared with Jesus.

Last Hours with Jesus

Jesus spoke to John and Peter. "Go and make ready for the Passover meal."

"Where shall we go?" they asked.

Jesus answered, "Go to Jerusalem and you will see a man carrying a pitcher of water. Follow him. Tell him the Master needs a room for the Passover meal. He will show you the place."

"I'm glad Jesus chose us for this job," John said to Peter as they hurried along.

They followed Jesus' instructions. Everything happened just like he had said

it would.

That same night Jesus came to the upper room with his disciples. John sat close to Jesus during the Passover meal. He felt uneasy when Jesus said, "One of you will betray me to the enemy." John knew he loved Jesus too much to do such a terrible thing.

"Who will it be?" they asked.

Then Jesus named his betrayer. It was Judas. Quietly Judas slipped out of the room.

Later the same evening Jesus took his disciples and went to the Mount of Olives. As they walked along there was a feeling of anxiety among them. The disciples were worried. They had seen and heard some of the religious leaders accusing and threatening Jesus.

When they reached the garden of Gethsemane Jesus said, "Sit here while I pray." Then he turned to John and Peter and James and said, "Come with me." The three looked at each other. They felt trouble was near. They were afraid, but they were glad to be near Jesus.

A little farther into the garden Jesus spoke again, "Wait here and watch." Then he went to pray alone.

As hard as they tried they could not stay awake. Jesus returned and found Peter and James and John sleeping. He asked, "Couldn't you stay awake and watch with me?"

They were ashamed of themselves. When Jesus left them they fell asleep again. But Jesus continued to pray.

Suddenly John awoke. He heard voices in the shadows. Judas came forward and kissed Jesus. The soldiers came out of the darkness and grabbed Jesus. They bound him and took him away.

John was afraid. "What will we do now?" he asked.

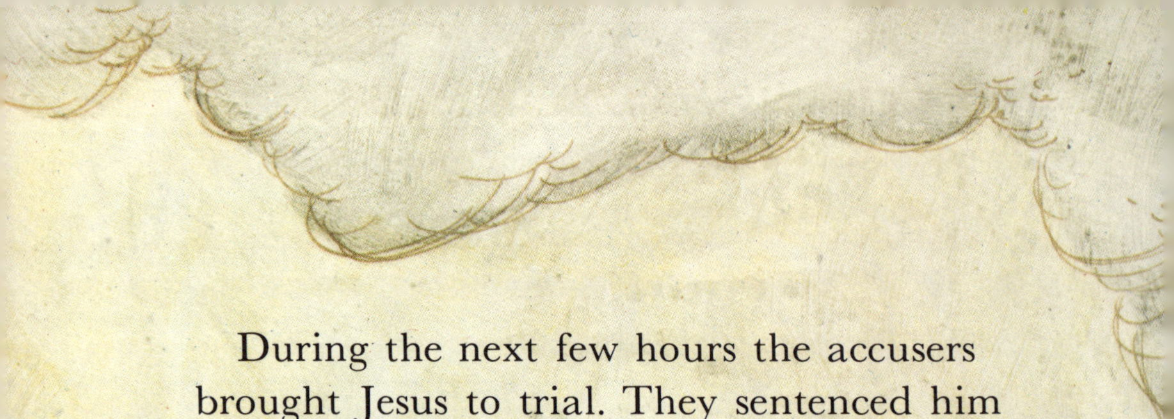

During the next few hours the accusers brought Jesus to trial. They sentenced him to die on the cross. Quickly the news of the crucifixion spread throughout the city.

John stood weeping at the foot of Jesus' cross. Standing with him in the crowd was Mary, the mother of Jesus. Jesus looked down and saw the two of them together. Jesus said to his mother, "Woman, here is your son." Then he looked at John and said, "Here is your mother."

From that moment on John took care of Mary. He took her to live in his own home.

The disciples were sad and lonely. Their Lord was dead. "If we only knew what to do," John said to Peter.

Jesus' body was buried in a tomb

carved from rock. On the third day after his death, some of the women went to the tomb.

"Peter! John! They have taken away the body of our Lord," the women cried as they came running from the tomb where Jesus had been buried.

Peter and John hurried to the tomb as fast as they could. John got there first but hesitated to enter. Peter rushed in. It was true. His body was gone. The news spread quickly.

It had happened as Jesus said. He rose from the dead on the third day. Soon he appeared to the women. Later he came to his disciples. John looked at him in

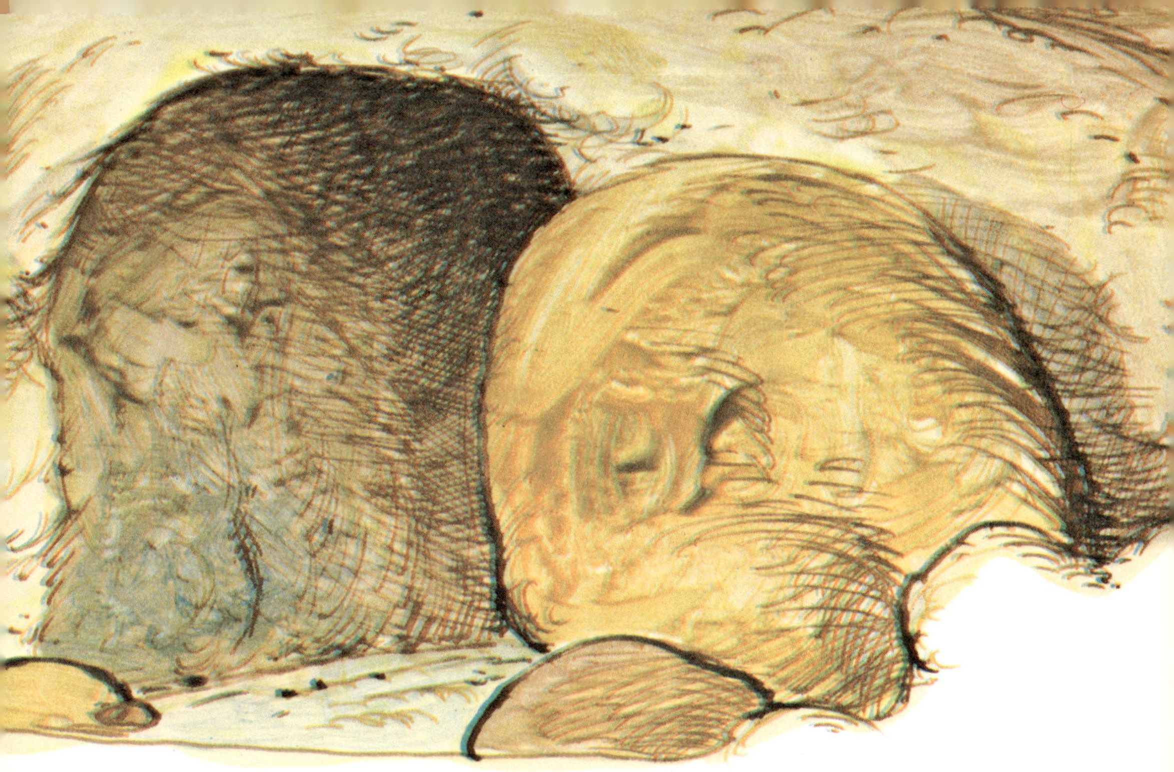

disbelief. He was overjoyed to be with his Master again.

Thinkback: What was the important assignment Jesus gave to John and Peter?

Whom did Jesus take to be close to him in the garden? Why do you think he chose those three?

How did the disciples feel when Jesus was crucified? How did they feel when he rose from the dead?

At Work for Jesus

The crowd filled the room where the disciples had gathered, but there was a feeling of emptiness. John felt lonely without Jesus.

After his resurrection Jesus spent forty days on earth. He appeared to his disciples many times during these days. Then he went to heaven to be with his heavenly Father.

Jesus' last command to his disciples was, "Go into all the world and preach the good news that I am alive."

John said to Peter, "The best place for us to begin preaching is right here in our own town."

They spoke boldly in the streets of Jerusalem. They said, "Turn away from your sins. Repent and believe in Jesus."

The people listened and many believed. Thousands were baptized.

One day John and his friend Peter went to the Temple. Outside the Beautiful Gate they saw a lame man begging.

"Give me some money," he asked.

They answered, "We do not have any silver or gold, but we have something far better to give you. In the name of Jesus, get up and walk."

The man jumped up and walked around. Jumping and praising God he followed John and Peter into the Temple. The people who saw him walking and rejoicing praised God with him.

John and Peter continued to preach and help people wherever they went. Many believed because of John's witness. One day as he and Peter preached, officers arrested them and put them in

prison. Soon John and Peter were out of prison and preaching again.

As John grew older he thought more and more about the three wonderful years he had spent with Jesus. He was glad he had left his fishing nets to follow Jesus. He remembered all of the things that had happened—the miracles, the crowds that followed Jesus, the accusers, his death, and his resurrection. John wanted all people to know and to love his beloved Savior, Jesus.

John wrote many of the things Jesus said and did. In his writings John said, "These are written that ye may believe that Jesus is the Christ, the Son of God; and that believing ye may have life in his name."

Thinkback: Jesus left work for his disciples to do. What was it?

Name some things John did to help others know about Jesus.

What books of the Bible have you read that John wrote?

Reflections

This page is to help you reflect or look back on the life of John, the beloved apostle. Look at these three important times in his life:

- John's call—"Come, follow me," Jesus said to John. Jesus wanted John to be his helper.
- John's training—Jesus had great plans for John. Jesus knew John would need training to carry out his work. Jesus taught John many important lessons.
- John's work—Jesus had work for John to do. This work was to tell others about Jesus. John was to tell about Jesus in word, in daily actions, and in writings.

Reflect on your own life. Consider

these same three important times in your life:

- My call—Jesus wants you to accept him as Savior and Lord of your life. He calls you to follow him.
- My training—Jesus wants you to learn the same lessons he taught John. You can do this by reading your Bible daily and by obeying God's teachings.
- My work—Jesus has work for you to do. He wants you to tell others about Jesus and his love.